The Social Action Manual

Six Steps to Repairing the World

Rabbi Noah Zvi Farkas

Editorial Committee

Nathan Weiner

Rabbi Evon Yakar

Dr. Ron Wolfson

BEHRMAN HOUSE, INC.

www.behrmanhouse.com

Book and Cover Design: LJ Graphics

Project Editor: Terry S. Kaye

Editorial Assistant: Wilhelmina Roepke

The publisher gratefully acknowledges the cooperation of the following sources of photographs for this book: David E. Behrman: 11; Eric Braun: front cover, right, 3, 16, 17, 38, 62, back cover, right; Gila Gevirtz: 12, 22; Terry S. Kaye: 14, 26, 50; Randi Simenhoff: front cover, left and bottom; Lisa F. Young (Shutterstock): back cover, left

———————————————————————————————

Library of Congress Cataloging-in-Publication Data

Farkas, Noah Zvi.
    The social action manual : six steps to repairing the world / Noah Zvi Farkas. p. cm.
  Includes bibliographical references and index.
ISBN 978-0-87441-773-9 (alk. paper)
1. Social action—Study and teaching. 2. Judaism and social problems—Study and teaching. 3. Helping behavior—Religious aspects—Judaism. 4. Jewish ethics—Study and teaching. I. Title.

    HN40.J5F37 2010
    296.3'80835—dc22

                                        2010006869

Letter from the Author   **4**

Workshop 1:   What Is Social Action?   **5**

Workshop 2:   Getting to the Issue   **13**

Workshop 3:   Looking for Needs to Choose a Project   **21**

Workshop 4:   Putting Your Project into Action   **33**

Workshop 5:   Doing and Assessing Your Project   **43**

Workshop 6:   Living a Life of Social Action   **53**

Conclusion   **62**

Letter from the Author

As a rabbi who cares deeply about the value of *tikun olam*—"repairing the world"—nothing is more important to me than engaging teenagers in social action. Through passion and hard work, you can make a difference in the world.

This handbook will expand your understanding of why doing social action is important and give you the tools to successfully plan, execute, and evaluate a social action project or initiative. Each workshop builds on the previous workshop to lead you through the entire process, all the while teaching skills about organizing and leadership. Along the way, you will learn Hebrew terms within social action, study Jewish texts that highlight social action, and read success stories of teenagers who created powerful social action initiatives. The final workshop will demonstrate that social action can actively involve you in Jewish communal life.

By embarking on a social action project or initiative, you will show you have chosen to take responsibility for your community and your world. I hope you find the process meaningful and fulfilling. May it lead you to better yourself and the world around you.

Rabbi Noah Zvi Farkas

What Is Social Action?

Objectives

By the end of this workshop you will be able to:

■ Define social action.

■ Explain the different models of social action.

■ Describe the Social Action Cycle.

Lesson Launch: Being a Guarantor

According to a midrash, when God was preparing to give the Torah to the Jewish people, God asked, "How do I know that the Jewish people will follow my Torah in every generation?"

Moses answered, "Because of their virtue, our ancestors will guarantee that the Jewish people will follow the Torah."

"But your ancestors are no longer living," said God.

So Moses said, "Because of their wisdom, the prophets and rabbis of Israel will guarantee that the Jewish people will follow the Torah."

"Not good enough," replied God.

Finally Moses said, "Our children will guarantee that the Jewish people will follow the Torah."

God said, "Yes. The children will be my guarantors."

In this midrash, why would God decide that the children—rather than the ancestors, prophets, and rabbis—will guarantee that the Jewish people follow the Torah?

_____

_____

_____

You, the young people of today, have the power to bring God into the world and to make a difference. But how can you take responsibility for big issues like poverty and injustice? Through social action! In this workshop you will learn about the different types of social action activities, as well as the cycle of social action projects and initiatives.

Focus on Text

תָּנוּ רַבָּנָן: בִּשְׁלֹשָׁה דְּבָרִים גְּדוֹלָה גְמִילוּת חֲסָדִים יוֹתֵר מִן הַצְּדָקָה.

Our rabbis taught: There are three ways in which acts of loving-kindness (ḥesed) are greater than giving tzedakah. One can only do tzedakah with money, while one can do ḥesed with time or money. One does tzedakah only toward the poor, while one does ḥesed for rich and poor alike. One does tzedakah only for the living, while one does ḥesed for both the living and the dead.

—Babylonian Talmud, Sukkah 49b

Do you think that acts of loving-kindness *(ḥesed)* are greater than acts of giving tzedakah? Explain your answer.

_____

_____

Name two examples of *ḥesed* that are not also tzedakah. Can you think of any types of tzedakah that do not also count as *ḥesed*? Which type is more difficult to list? Why?

_____

_____

Acts of *ḥesed* require passion, time, and energy. The rabbis point out that charitable giving is important, but unlike tzedakah, *ḥesed* gives everyone an opportunity to help others, even those of us who lack resources or do not feel powerful.

What Is Social Action?

The twentieth-century social theorist Max Weber described social action as the kinds of interactions between people that *change* the way humanity lives. Over time, the term "social action" evolved to mean the different types of activities that *improve* the way humanity lives. These activities include philanthropy (giving money), direct service, advocacy, activism, and community organizing.

Types of Social Action

PHILANTHROPY (GIVING MONEY)

Money can help improve the world when you donate it or use it to fund charitable organizations. When you give money directly to those in need, you can aid them with their immediate problems. When you help people to buy food, for example, you are providing them with what they most need to survive. Giving money to a cause, such as an advocacy group or a direct service initiative like a food shelter, is another good way to show your concern. Without donor support, social service organizations like the Jewish Federation or the Salvation Army could not exist. But giving, whether to individuals or to organizations, is not always sustainable. Alleviating an immediate problem, by providing food for a day or paying an aid worker's salary for the month, may not address the reasons for these needs. The people you are helping may still have the same needs after the money is gone. Philanthropy is most successful when one gives regularly to a specific cause.

DIRECT SERVICE

You can give your time to help others through direct service programs such as soup kitchens, food banks, and homeless shelters. You can tutor individuals who need academic support, or you can build houses for the homeless or the victims of natural disasters. Providing service to another person is a way to give back to your community and to interact directly with those in need. But direct service, like giving money, does not address the root causes of problems. Though it provides tangible results, direct service rarely solves a social issue.

ADVOCACY

The goal of advocacy is to change public policy in order to help a specific group of people. The advocate represents that group in front of government officials, the media, or other interested individuals. For example, Jewish World Watch is an organization that advocates on behalf of the victims of genocide in Darfur through letter-writing campaigns, media interviews, and school programming. Successful advocacy requires many hours of time and dedication.

ACTIVISM

Marches, protests, advertising and petitions are the most common avenues for activism. In the 1960s, the civil rights movement drew attention to the inequality of rights and services for African Americans by staging marches through the South and sit-ins at segregated lunch counters. These activities raised an awareness that eventually led to the change of discriminatory laws. Protests and rallies are more unpredictable than other means of social change, and they have in the past led to violence between groups on different sides of the issues.

COMMUNITY ORGANIZING

Community organizing mobilizes groups of people to achieve positive social change. For example, recently the Greater Boston Interfaith Organization (GBIO) won affordable health care for tens of thousands of working families. Organizing is most effective when leaders try to create change within their own community. Community organizations include labor unions, nonprofits, groups of businesses, and coalitions of churches, synagogues, and mosques.

Organizing can be the most sustainable avenue of social change, because it seeks to solve the root problems of society, such as winning access to quality and affordable housing, health care, and education. It is also the most costly and lengthy process of social change.

Match each social action project to its corresponding type.
(*Hint*: there can be more than one answer for each project.)

_____ 1. Serving soup at a community kitchen.

_____ 2. Collecting coats to distribute to the poor or homeless.

_____ 3. Speaking about bullying to your principal on behalf of a friend.

_____ 4. Organizing a rally for Israel.

_____ 5. Raising money for cancer research.

_____ 6. Gathering community members to ask for a stop sign on a street corner to prevent accidents.

_____ 7. Building a house for the homeless.

_____ 8. Writing letters to a congressman about protecting the environment.

_____ 9. Holding a food drive.

_____ 10. Visiting a friend in the hospital.

_____ 11. Selling rubber bracelets to increase awareness of genocide.

_____ 12. Sponsoring a dance-a-thon to benefit AIDS victims.

A.	Philanthropy
B.	Direct Service
C.	Advocacy
D.	Activism
E.	Community Organizing

The Social Action Cycle

Every social action project or initiative, whether it is philanthropy, direct service, advocacy, activism, or community organizing, follows the same cycle. Each project or initiative begins with a clear plan, followed by the social action itself, and it ends with an evaluation of the project. You can remember the cycle by focusing on three words: **PLAN. ACT. EVALUATE.**

PLAN

The plan is the foundation for every successful social action project. A good plan contains measurable goals such as collecting a specific amount of money, planting a certain number of trees, or hosting a rally. Social action plans also give focus to a project or initiative by establishing timelines, lists of materials, and participant turnout, to keep you on track to reach your goals. Workshops 2 and 3 will teach you how to plan a project or initiative in detail.

ACT

This is the center of your social action project. It is here that you carry out your plan.

EVALUATE

Evaluating your project helps you to determine how effective it was (How many people did you serve? Did you raise enough money? Did you change social policy?) and what you need to do to be even more successful in the future. You will learn more about evaluating your social action project or initiative in Workshop 5.

The Social Action Cycle

ACT

PLAN

EVALUATE

HEBREW HELPER

תִּקּוּן עוֹלָם *(Tikun Olam)* **Repairing the World**

According to the Jewish mystical tradition, when God created the world, millions of sparks of divine light escaped across all of creation. It is the task of the Jewish people to gather the sparks back together. When we perform *mitzvot*, we collect the sparks and lift them up to light the world. This is called making a *tikun*, or "repair." When we help others through social action we can repair the brokenness of the world one spark at a time.

Social Action Notebook: Making Social Action Jewish

Many leaders who effect real social change are motivated by their faith. Martin Luther King Jr., a religious leader and civil rights activist, saw his faith as the cornerstone of his activism. While in prison for his activism he wrote, "...just as the Apostle Paul left his village of Tarsus and carried the gospel of Jesus Christ to the far corners of the Greco-Roman world, so am I compelled to carry the gospel of freedom far beyond my own hometown...." ("Letter from Birmingham Jail") Reverend King believed that when he spoke out for civil rights he was living his Christianity.

Use the following guide to help find what makes social action Jewish to you.

In what ways is social action Jewish?

_____

_____

Rabbi Abraham Joshua Heschel was involved in the civil rights movement. Upon his return from a march with Martin Luther King Jr. he said, "I felt as though my legs were praying." What do you think Rabbi Heschel meant by that statement?

_____

_____

Write your own covenant for a commitment to social action.

_____

_____

_____

Real World

Sejal Hathi, Girls Helping Girls

Sejal Hathi of Fremont, California, always enjoyed helping others. As a teenager she saw the wide gap between girls in wealthy countries and girls in developing countries. Inspired by her experiences with a nonprofit organization called Girls for a Change, Sejal, then fifteen, founded the organization Girls Helping Girls, to pair teams of girls in the developed world with teams of girls in developing countries to promote education, organizing, and communal development through microlending projects. To date, Sejal's organization has helped over five thousand girls in fifteen countries by providing scholarships, books, food, and water.

What gap is Sejal trying to close? How is she successful?

_____

_____

What types of social action does she employ?

_____

_____

Reflections

In this workshop you have learned the definition of social action, the different types of social action, and the Social Action Cycle. You have also learned a few Hebrew terms associated with social action. Before you plan a social action project, reflect on this workshop by answering the following questions.

1. Of the types of social action (philanthropy, direct service, advocacy, activism, and community organizing), which one seems easiest to you? Which seems hardest? Why?

    _____

    _____

    _____

2. What are some of the needs in your community or in the world that you think you could help address?

    _____

    _____

    _____

Getting to the Issue

Objectives

By the end of this workshop you will be able to:

- Explain your reasons and motivation for doing social action.
- Describe social problems in terms of solvable social issues.
- Begin to consider projects or initiatives that address social issues.

Lesson Launch: Climbing a Mountain

There is a proverb that asks: "How do you climb a mountain?"

Answer: "One step at a time."

Often large problems seem too big to tackle. It is best to break them down into smaller parts and work on each part individually. For high school students, the prospect of applying to college, for example, can be overwhelming. However, if you break the process down into smaller components, such as writing an essay, securing transcripts, and asking your teachers or rabbi for a letter of recommendation, you can easily complete the task in the same way you climb a mountain—one step at a time.

Describe a time recently when you felt overwhelmed by the number of things you had to do. Perhaps it was the amount of homework, number of extra-curricular activities, or family obligations. What did you do to feel more in control?

_____

_____

In this workshop you will learn about taking large social problems and breaking them down into workable social issues. You will also learn ways of turning social issues into social action projects or initiatives. These steps are an essential beginning to the social action planning process.

Focus on Text

כִּי לֹא־יֶחְדַּל אֶבְיוֹן מִקֶּרֶב הָאָרֶץ עַל־כֵּן אָנֹכִי מְצַוְּךָ לֵאמֹר פָּתֹחַ תִּפְתַּח אֶת־יָדְךָ לְאָחִיךָ לַעֲנִיֶּךָ וּלְאֶבְיֹנֶךָ . . .

Because there will always be poor in the midst of the land, I command you, saying: open your hand to your brother, to your needy, and to your poor....

—*Deuteronomy 15:11*

רַבִּי טַרְפוֹן אוֹמֵר. . . הוּא הָיָה אוֹמֵר לֹא עָלֶיךָ הַמְּלָאכָה לִגְמוֹר וְלֹא אַתָּה בֶּן־חוֹרִין לְהִבָּטֵל מִמֶּנָּה.

Rabbi Tarfon used to say... "It is not your duty to finish the task, but you are not free to give up either."

—*Pirkei Avot 2:21*

These texts seem to say that the Jewish tradition sees no end to poverty. Why do you think this is so?

_____

_____

According to the quotes above, how does Judaism want us to respond to the poor? Do you agree with this response? Why or why not?

_____

_____

_____

_____

_____

_____

Who Am I?

Reflect on your motivations for doing social action by answering the questions that follow.

1. Describe an experience where you felt you were helpful to a person or animal in need. How did you help? How did you feel afterward?

_____

_____

_____

2. Why did you decide to be helpful?

_____

_____

When you make a difference in the world, you make a difference in yourself. Thinking back on your own experiences of helping others, you can find out more about what kind of person you are. By doing social action and concentrating on improving the lives and opportunities of the needy in your community, you can become more compassionate and generous.

WE CAN'T SOLVE PROBLEMS, BUT WE CAN WORK ON ISSUES

When you hear a news reporter say that thousands of people are hungry or homeless in America, you might say, "What can I do? I'm just one person, and these problems are too big to solve." You're right. Social problems *are* too big to solve. Instead it helps to think in terms of social *issues*. What is the difference?

Social problems are *impersonal* or *abstract* society ills, such as poverty, drug abuse, and hunger. These problems are unattached to any particular person or place.

Write down other impersonal or abstract social problems.

_____

_____

With social problems, it's difficult to measure success. For example, at what point can we say that we have solved the problem of poverty? What we call poor today might be different from what our grandparents considered poor. As our standards and perspectives change, our ability to measure abstract problems also shifts. For this reason we can say that social problems are unsolvable.

Social issues, on the other hand, are measurable. We know how many people we can feed today or how to increase wages for workers in our town. Because social issues are *personal*, we can do specific things to help. Good social action projects and initiatives focus on specific issues, not on large abstract problems. Because social issues are personal and have measurable goals for success, we can say they are solvable.

FINDING THE ISSUE

In order to effect social change we try to transform abstract problems into specific issues. We do this by asking three simple questions: **Who? Where? Why?** Let's use hunger as an example.

Who? The problem of hunger is abstract. Transform this problem into an issue by asking, *Who is affected by hunger?* Is it the elderly? New immigrants? The answer will tell you where you can start a project or a campaign. Once you know *who* they are, you can then plan how to help them.

Where? In order to move from an abstract problem to a specific issue find out where those in need live. Do the hungry live in your neighborhood? Do they attend your school or your synagogue? Do they live in another part of your city? Once you know *where* they live, you can design projects or initiatives that are appropriate for the location.

Why? We can transform a social problem into a social issue by looking for the causes that led to the problem in the first place. Are the elderly unable to get to the store to buy food? Are the new immigrants unfamiliar with food stamps and other social services? Once you know the *why* you can address the specific issue and try to change it.

Getting to the Issue

Practice turning abstract problems into solvable issues. Ask, *Who? Where?* and *Why?* in order to change social problems into social issues.

Social Problem	Questions	Social Issue
Hunger	Who?	New immigrants
	Where?	In my town
	Why?	High cost of living and unemployment.
Illegal drug use	Who?	_____
	Where?	_____
	Why?	_____
_____	Who?	_____
	Where?	_____
	Why?	_____

Social Action Notebook:
Issues to Projects

Now that we have filtered abstract social problems into specific social issues, we can take those social issues and translate them into social action projects and initiatives.

In Workshop One we learned that there are five primary types of social action: **Philanthropy (Giving Money), Direct Service, Advocacy, Activism, and Community Organizing.** Look at this example that translates an issue into social action projects.

Example:

Some members of our community cannot afford to buy enough healthy food to feed their families.

Philanthropy:	Raise money for a local charity that feeds the hungry.
Direct Service:	Work at a soup kitchen or food pantry.
Advocacy:	Take a group of peers to city hall to lobby on behalf of the families in need.
Activism:	Organize a demonstration that educates the public about the families in need.
Community Organizing:	Organize the families who need food assistance to demand better service from the government.

Look back at the reflection questions on page 12 and think of ways to translate the community needs you picked into social action projects or initiatives. By brainstorming at least one example of each, you will probably think of more than one initiative on which you would like to work.

The issue I am exploring is: _____

Philanthropy: _____

Direct Service: _____

Advocacy: _____

Activism: _____

Community Organizing: _____

HEBREW HELPER

נוֹתֵן לֶחֶם לָרְעֵבִים (*Notein Leḥem La're'eivim*) Feeding the Hungry

According to the Talmud, Rabbi Huna left his door open to welcome those without food, saying, "All who are hungry come and eat." Centuries later, we speak these words at every Passover seder. However, the hungry are in need of food all through the year. Many synagogues and communities support local food pantries and soup kitchens, and also raise funds for and awareness about global hunger.

Real World

David Levitt, Cafeteria Harvester

David Levitt was a sixth-grade student in Tampa Bay, Florida. He was also a year away from becoming a bar mitzvah. David cared very much about hunger in his community. Not sure how to help, he devoted his bar mitzvah project to learning more about this problem.

David discovered that the local soup kitchen had to turn away fifty people a day because there was not enough room or money to feed them. He found a local organization, Tampa Bay Harvest, that collects prepared food and donates it to shelters and soup kitchens. David petitioned the school board and the superintendent of his school district to work with Tampa Bay Harvest to donate cafeteria food to local shelters and soup kitchens. The first year, the school donated 55,000 pounds of food to shelters. By the time David turned fifteen, all ninety-two schools in his district participated in the program, donating 255,906 pounds of food annually to shelters. When David graduated from high school, the program had spread to all the public schools in Florida, which donated annually over 1,000,000 pounds of food.

How did David translate the *problem* of hunger into a solvable *issue*?

_____

_____

What types of social action projects did David work on to help solve this issue?

_____

_____

Reflections

In this workshop you learned how to translate large, abstract social problems into workable social issues by personalizing them. You have also begun the work of identifying social issues and thinking about possible projects that address those issues.

Before choosing a project, reflect on this workshop by considering how you might become a better person through social action. What might you learn from doing social action? How might you grow?

_____

_____

_____

_____

_____

_____

_____

_____

_____

_____

_____

Looking for Needs to Choose a Project

Objectives

By the end of this workshop you will be able to:

■ Determine which social problems you are passionate about.

■ Identify some of the social needs of your own community.

■ Decide on a social action project.

Lesson Launch: Social Action Quiz

When doing social action, it is best to first identify what social issues concern you. Take this social action quiz by ranking your feelings in response to these situations, where 1 does not bother you very much and 5 bothers you a lot.

	Does not bother me				Bothers me a lot
1. You see litter on the sidewalk or notice someone tossing trash out of a car window.	1	2	3	4	5
2. You learn that the polar bear was added to the endangered species list.	1	2	3	4	5
3. There seem to be more and more news stories about climate change and global warming.	1	2	3	4	5
4. You see a homeless person asking for money.	1	2	3	4	5
5. There are people you know who do not have a Shabbat meal because they can't afford one.	1	2	3	4	5
6. There are children in the local hospital who miss their friends.	1	2	3	4	5
7. A report in the newspaper gives the latest death toll for people with AIDS in Africa.	1	2	3	4	5
8. You see stray cats and dogs in the neighborhood with no one to care for them.	1	2	3	4	5
9. After a storm or earthquake, there are people without food, water, or shelter.	1	2	3	4	5

Look at your score:

- If you circled a 3 or higher on questions 1, 2, and 3, you are probably concerned about the environment.

- If you circled 3 or higher on question 4, 5, and 9, you are probably concerned about poverty and hunger.

- If you circled 3 or higher on 6 and 7, you are probably concerned about how the sick are cared for.

- If you circled 3 or higher on questions 2 and 8, you are probably concerned about the welfare of animals.

- If you circled 3 or higher on questions 7 and 9, you are probably concerned about disaster response.

Write down your area of greatest concern.

_____

Explain why you feel strongly about this area.

_____

_____

A long list of concerns can seem unmanageable and make you feel hopeless. Now that you have a short list, you can begin to focus on projects that are specific to what you care about most. In this workshop you will learn how to find out more about what motivates you, what the needs are of a particular community, and what resources are in place to help address those needs.

Focus on Text

פָּתֹחַ תִּפְתַּח אֶת־יָדְךָ לְאָחִיךָ לַעֲנִיֶּךָ וּלְאֶבְיֹנְךָ, לָמָּה נֶאֶמְרוּ כֻּלָּם הָרָאוּי לְתֵן לוֹ פַּת נוֹתְנִים לוֹ פַּת עִסָּה נוֹתְנִים לוֹ עִסָּה.

You will open your hand to your fellow, to your poor. To the one who needs bread give bread, to the one who needs dough give dough.

—*Sifrei Deuteronomy 118*

Jewish tradition makes it clear that it is our responsibility to help the poor.

What can you learn from this quote about the needs of different people and how we should respond?

_____

_____

When we do social action, we must first be aware of the needs in a community and then determine how best to meet those needs. This needs-based approach changes our orientation from "What do I want to do?" to "What needs to be done?"

ASSESSING NEEDS

Jewish tradition teaches that, "There will always be poor in the midst of the land" (Deuteronomy 15:11). How can you help the needy most effectively? In order to do any social action project well, you should find out about the needs of the community you wish to help. The process of looking for what is needed is called doing a "needs assessment."

WHAT IS A NEED?

A "need" can mean the gap between the way things are and the way we want them to be. A need can affect an individual, a group of individuals, or the entire community. Since the members of our communities are diverse, their needs are likely to be equally diverse. Older community members, for example, might need help getting to the grocery store to buy food, while mothers with young children may need childcare in order to get their shopping done. Teachers might need filing cabinets or bookshelves for their classroom, whereas students need pencils and desks. Looking for needs is the first step toward finding solutions to problems.

IDENTIFYING NEEDS

Identifying needs is one of the most important steps in the process of doing social action, because when we are looking for needs, we are preparing to solve social issues. You can identify needs in many ways, including holding small group meetings or interviewing community members. Here are a few other ways to look for needs:

- *Read the synagogue bulletin or school newsletter.* Often synagogues and schools print community events and requests for volunteers in their weekly or monthly newsletters. Check out who is in the hospital or who is in need of some friendly help because of poor health or a new baby in the family.

- *Talk to community leaders like the rabbi, education director, or your teacher.* Community leaders can help you identify pressing needs.

- *Talk to other community members.* Community members of different ages have different life experiences and can give you ideas of how to serve your community. Perhaps you will encounter someone who volunteered in their youth registering African American voters in the South or who immigrated to America with the help of a social service organization.

- *Talk to your family members.* Ask your family what they care about and if they know of anyone in the community that might need help.

- *Talk to your friends.* Some of your friends may already have done social action work and can give you ideas about projects they have enjoyed or found meaningful.

- *Visit movement-based Web sites.* Search social justice and legislative action Web sites for areas of need. For example, the Religious Action Center in Washington, D.C. offers a social action program bank with thousands of ideas and programs that have been successfully implemented in Reform congregations. The United Synagogue of Conservative Judaism and the Jewish Reconstructionist Federation provide extensive resources and social action initiatives too.

- *Hold a focus group.* Gather a small group (ten or fewer people) at the synagogue or in someone's home in order to discuss a particular topic, like unemployment. You may want to ask your rabbi, education director, or parent to suggest interested individuals. Use this opportunity to get to know members of the community in an informal setting. By inviting a diverse group, you can get a better picture of the needs of the community.

Needs Assessment Interview

Sometimes speaking with adults about social action, especially your parent, the rabbi, cantor, or the education director, can be difficult. This interview form with sample questions will help guide you. You can use it both in one-on-one interviews and as a guideline for hosting a focus group.

Needs Assessment Interview Form

Person's name:_____

Position (Rabbi, Cantor, Education Director, Synagogue Member, etc.):

_____

_____

I would like to do a social action project in our community. As part of the project, I am interviewing people to see what needs might be filled through social action. Do you mind if I ask you a few questions?

1. What are some of the needs in our community?

_____

_____

2. What do we already do to address those needs?

_____

_____

3. What resources does our community have to meet those needs?

_____

_____

4. What resources are missing?

_____

_____

FOUR HANDY TIPS FOR GATHERING INFORMATION:

1. *Write everything down.* As you conduct your interviews and talk to community members, make sure to write down what you learn. This is especially true when you do research about the resources available in your community.

2. *Start with what you know.* For example, if you already know that there is a local hospital that specializes in pediatric medicine, you can then interview a community member to find out if they have a peer tutoring program to help hospitalized children with school work, or a pet companion program to give the children time to play with a dog or cat. By beginning in a place where you feel comfortable with the information you already know, you can expand your knowledge to find possible needs in the community.

3. *Focus on targets.* When you do a needs assessment, think of the people that would be helped by a project. Who are they? Where do they live? In what ways would the project help them?

4. *Identify the people who can help you fill in missing information.* Often the missing link in your search for needs will be easy to find if you just keep asking, "Who knows the answers to my questions?" For example, if you are considering helping out in a hospital, you might wonder if the hospital has a peer tutoring or pet companion program. Who is likely to have that information? You could call the hospital volunteer services department to ask them, or there might be a doctor or nurse who belongs to your synagogue or a parent in your school who knows.

Be sure to review your needs assessment more than once during each step of your project. It will help you focus on the issues your project should address and keep you on track.

Moving Forward

Gather the information you have collected from your interviews and observations. Include the needs you plan to address, ideas for possible projects or initiatives, and the resources that you currently have (such as time, useful contacts, or willing volunteers). Then answer the following questions.

1. What do I already know about my project or initiative?

2. What do I still need to know?

3. Who can help me with my project or initiative?

Choosing a Project or Initiative

In the previous workshops you learned about the different types of social action and about how to translate large social problems into specific social action projects. In this workshop, you assessed the needs in your community. Now you will take all of this information and use it to choose the social action project that is right for you.

You learned in Workshop 1 that Rabbi Abraham Joshua Heschel teaches that doing social action is a Jewish thing. Below is a list of *mitzvot* (commandments) that express social action ideas in a Jewish way. Use this list to brainstorm possible projects. Then add your own ideas for doing social action.

Protecting the Environment *(Bal Tashḥit)*

- Volunteer to clean up local parks, beaches, rivers, or nature preserves.
- Start a campaign to use compact fluorescent light bulbs, reusable water bottles, or canvas tote bags.
- Advocate for more open spaces in urban environments.
- Other:_____

Visiting the Sick *(Bikur Ḥolim)*

- Visit community members at a hospital, convalescent center, assisted living facility, or nursing home.
- Arrange to take pets to hospitals to visit patients.
- Raise money for cancer research or another health-related cause.
- Other:_____

Feeding the Hungry *(Notein Leḥem La're'eivim)*

- Raise money or collect packaged foods to give to a soup kitchen or food pantry.
- Volunteer at local soup kitchens or food pantries.
- Help those who are hungry to sign up for food assistance programs.
- Other:_____

Fighting Genocide *(Lo Taḥmod)*

- Volunteer with a nonprofit organization whose mission is to fight genocide.

- Participate in an oral history project with survivors of genocide.

- Start a campaign to encourage local businesses not to do business with countries that support genocide.

- Other:_____

Compassion for Animals *(Tza'ar Ba'alei Ḥayim)*

- Volunteer at an animal shelter.

- Host a pet adoption day at your synagogue or school.

- Start a campaign for purchasing only free-range products like eggs, chicken, or beef.

- Other:_____

Clothing the Naked *(Malbish Arumim)*

- Start a clothing drive for items such as coats, shoes, and eyeglasses, and donate them to local organizations.

- Ask local clothing stores to contribute gift certificates so that victims of domestic violence can afford to buy nice clothes for themselves and their children.

- Knit caps and blankets for Israeli soldiers.

- Other:_____

Fighting Homelessness *(Shikun L'ḥasrei Bayit)*

- Volunteer at a homeless shelter.

- Raise money to support local nonprofit organizations whose mission is to fight homelessness.

- Start a letter-writing campaign to advocate for the homeless in your area.

- Other:_____

Social Action Notebook:
Putting It All Together

Use the following worksheet to decide what your social action project or initiative will be. Refer back to the previous workshops to review all the information you have gathered.

My passion is:

_____

A social issue that I can help solve is:

_____

The specific needs I will address are:

_____

The current resources available are:

_____

My project or initiative will be:

_____

_____

_____

Real World

Shifra, the Soup Kitchen Seamstress

During a class visit to a soup kitchen, Shifra Mincer, a sixth grader in New York, noticed that many of the people at the kitchen wore torn jackets, pants, and shirts. When one of the patrons of the kitchen asked if anyone knew how to sew, Shifra spoke up and said that she did. She sat at a table with a sewing kit and began to mend the ripped clothing of the homeless at the soup kitchen. Shifra returned the next week to continue mending clothes. For nearly six years, Shifra came back week after week to sew the clothes of those in need.

Several years later when Shifra was sixteen, a teacher at her Jewish high school in New York asked Shifra if her skills as a seamstress could bring comfort to children in the hospital. Shifra reached out to friends and started a sewing club to make heart-shaped pillows for the sick children. They later expanded the project to the adult residents of a local nursing home. Shifra and her fellow club members wrote letters and made announcements in her high school and synagogue community asking for donations of materials and sewing machines. Shifra has helped thousands of people in her community.

What needs did Shifra initially identify? How did she identify them?

_____

Over time, Shifra's work expanded beyond the soup kitchen. How did she adjust to her changing opportunities?

_____

_____

HEBREW HELPER

בְּקוּר חוֹלִים (Bikur Ḥolim) Visiting the Sick

According to the rabbis, three angels visited Abraham while he was convalescing (Genesis 18). Visitors bring comfort and companionship to those who are sick. Many communities have volunteers who go to hospitals or make phone calls to the sick. Such volunteers often report feeling closer to their community after these visits. Visiting the sick regularly is one way to help build a compassionate community and incorporate social action into your life.

Reflections

In this workshop you learned how to identify your own passions for social action and how to focus on areas of concern. You have also learned about the needs of your community by doing a needs assessment. Using that information, you had the opportunity to choose a project or initiative that is both meaningful to you and the community.

Write down your thoughts about moving forward and doing a social action project. What are your greatest worries? What are you most excited about? How will you know that you have succeeded?

_____

_____

_____

_____

_____

_____

_____

Putting Your Project into Action

By the end of this workshop you will be able to:

■ Set a schedule for your project or initiative.

■ Recruit others to help.

■ Publicize your project or initiative.

■ Manage a group of volunteers.

Lesson Launch: Time Management

Imagine your typical school day. What is your schedule? What things do you need with you throughout the day? Whom do you meet? Jot down your typical schedule here:

My Typical Daily Schedule:

7:00 AM	_____
8:00	_____
9:00	_____
10:00	_____
11:00	_____
12:00 PM	_____
1:00	_____
2:00	_____
3:00	_____
4:00	_____
5:00	_____
6:00	_____

What I Take to School:

_____

_____

_____

_____

_____

I Am Meeting:

1)

2)

3)

Setting schedules, listing materials, and contacting others are all important parts of doing social action. In this workshop you will learn how to develop a timetable for your project, recruit others, and publicize your project.

Focus on Text

כָּבֵד מִמְּךָ הַדָּבָר לֹא־תוּכַל עֲשֹׂהוּ לְבַדֶּךָ. . .

...The job is too heavy for you; you can't do it alone!

—Exodus 18:18

When the Israelites wandered in the desert, Moses sat as a judge over all the people from morning until night. After an especially hard day, Jethro, Moses' father-in-law, came to him and said, "What are you doing? Don't you know you are going to wear yourself out?"

Moses responded that, as the leader, he had to teach the people how to behave. But Jethro told him, "This is not right—the burden is too much for one person. Instead, appoint trusted representatives to help you in the disputes of the people. That way you only have to deal with the most important matters. You can empower others to be leaders, and you can go home and sleep at night."

When you do social action, it is important to recruit volunteers and delegate tasks to other people. Planning and executing a project on your own can be complicated—and exhausting. By adding people to your project, you can share the responsibility of the workload and invite others to take ownership of the project with you.

List the tasks that need to be done for your social action project or initiative.

1._____   4._____

2._____   5._____

3._____   6._____

Which of these tasks must be completed by you?

1._____   3._____

2._____

Which of these tasks can be completed by someone else?

1._____   3._____

2._____

Social Action Notebook:
Building Your Project or Initiative

Let's look back at the Social Action Cycle. The cycle has three parts: PLAN, ACT, and EVALUATE. So far you have been deep in the planning process. You looked at the social problems and social issues in your community and balanced them with the resources available. Now you are ready to act. You can use the following worksheet to bring focus to your project or initiative.

MY SOCIAL ACTION PROJECT

I hope to achieve:

_____

_____

My project is:

_____

I will launch my project on (date):

_____

The location of my project is:

_____

The address is:

_____

_____

Materials I need for my project are:

_____

_____

_____

My primary contact person is: _____

His/her e-mail and phone number are: _____

Things I need help with and who can help me:

_____

_____

SETTING A TIMETABLE

Now that you have chosen a project or initiative and have begun brainstorming the different tasks and materials you need, create a timetable for the period from now until the day you expect to implement your plan. Be sure to allow ample time for developing the project in order to recruit enough volunteers and create enough publicity.

List what needs to be accomplished ONE MONTH before the project or initiative.

_____

_____

List what needs to be accomplished ONE WEEK before the project or initiative.

_____

_____

List what needs to be accomplished ONE DAY before the project or initiative.

_____

_____

ASSESSMENT BREAK

Assessment or evaluation is a key part of the Social Action Cycle. Be sure to evaluate at every stage, not just after the project or initiative is completed. What have you done well until now? What could you do better as you enter into the final stages of planning? Write your reflections here.

_____

_____

_____

_____

_____

WHOM TO RECRUIT

When doing social action, try to recruit from a broad base of people. Different volunteers can bring different skills to your project or initiative, such as the ability to drive, to create a Web site for you, or to draw or paint posters and flyers. Think of your project. Write down who from each group might be helpful to you and why.

Your family:

_____

_____

Your friends:

_____

_____

Your synagogue clergy and staff:

_____

_____

GATHER YOUR VOLUNTEERS

Every social action project requires a team of people working together as a community in order for it to be successful. Whether they are your family, friends, or people you have met during the planning process, each person you recruit to your project relieves the amount of work you have to do as an organizer. You may even turn them on to doing social action! Here are some general tips for recruiting volunteers:

- *Make sure the goals of your project are clear.* Your goals should be short, direct, and simple. This lets volunteers know what level of commitment you are expecting from them. For example, you can say, "I hope to collect one hundred blankets and distribute them to homeless shelters this winter. I'll need help distributing the blankets on Sunday afternoon." This gives your potential volunteers an understanding of the project, its time frame, and the type of help you might expect from them.

- *Always be polite.* When you ask people to donate their time and energy, be sure to ask nicely and to thank them for their efforts. This will go a long way toward making them feel good about their commitment and helping you get the job done.

- *Ask for specific commitments, not general assurances.* When asking volunteers for their help, say, "Can you work three hours next week in the late afternoon and early evening?" not simply, "Can you help me out?" By being specific, you signal to the volunteers that you are respectful of their time.

- *"No" does not always mean "never."* If you keep your commitments specific, then when potential volunteers say "no" to you, they are not refusing to help completely. Ask if there is some other way they can help. Can they commit to calling five people about the project rather than ten? Can they help on a different day? Perhaps they can come to your venue for just a few minutes to give support to the other volunteers? If they continue to say "no," then move on to someone else.

Publicity: Get the Word Out

Publicize your project or initiative so that people will know what you are doing and why it is important. Through publicity you can also recruit volunteers, raise money, and increase participation. Check off below the avenues for publicity that interest you, then add your own ideas.

- ❏ Create an attractive flyer and post copies in your school, synagogue, local coffee shop, or supermarket.

- ❏ Write a letter to local officials and businesses asking for their support.

- ❏ Write a paragraph describing your project that can be put in the weekly announcements or on the Web site of your school or synagogue.

- ❏ Write an article about your project and submit it to your school newspaper, synagogue bulletin or a local publication.

- ❏ Write a short text or e-mail message inviting your friends and classmates to help out.

- ❏ Call community members to tell them about the project and invite them to attend or help out.

- ❏ Create a page on Facebook or MySpace or create your own Web site where participants can find updates and other information.

- ❏ My own idea: _____

YOUR MESSAGE

Use the following space to write a short paragraph describing who you are, what your project or initiative is, why it is important, and what support you might need from other people. You can then use this paragraph as a base from which you can recruit volunteers, ask for support, write an article for your local newspaper, and do outreach to the broader community.

_____

_____

_____

_____

_____

SIX STEPS TO MAKING A GREAT POSTER OR FLYER

Use these proven techniques for creating attention-grabbing posters and flyers and you will see big results in your marketing efforts.

1. Write a snappy phrase or headline.

Use unusual words and pop culture references that draw people to your poster or flyer. Phrases like "Refugee Relief," "Act Now," and "Stand Up" are some examples of attention-getting language.

2. Use colorful or striking graphics.

One large image will have more impact than many smaller images. This image is your focal point and will serve as the anchor for your work. The image should be high quality and clear to your readers. If you are on a tight printing or photocopying budget, try using colored paper instead of color graphics. Simply print with black ink on colored paper and use grey tones to add texture.

3. Organize your page.

You do not need to fill your poster or flyer with complicated text and graphics. Allowing white space will make important elements stand out and the piece easy to read.

4. Focus on the good stuff.

Show your readers the benefits of volunteering for the project. Use positive words like "meaningful," "opportunity," and "exciting" to convey your message. Be sure to keep your text short and to the point.

5. Use testimonials.

Connect your readers to the project by including endorsements from appreciative people associated with the issue. With their permission, include their names and how they are connected with the project.

6. Don't forget to proofread!

Check and double-check your poster or flyer. Have someone else proofread your work. Check your contact information, date, and location of the project. Test the phone numbers or go to the Web site to make sure that all your links work.

Shelby, the Jeweler for Women in Darfur

When Shelby Layne, a high school student in Los Angeles, California, learned of the genocide in Darfur, she knew she wanted to take action. Her father told her about Jewish World Watch (JWW), a California-based organization whose goal is to fight against genocide and human rights violations, and she became deeply interested in the subject.

Shelby learned that Darfuri women living in refugee camps would risk their lives to leave the camps and collect firewood from the unprotected countryside in order to cook food for their families. To protect against these risks, Jewish World Watch developed the Solar Cooker Project to provide cooking units that harness the energy of the sun rather than firewood. In partnership with JWW, Shelby looked for a way to raise money to pay for the construction and shipping of solar cookers.

She asked herself, "What skills do I have?" Shelby is an amateur jewelry maker. She asked her friends and family to donate jewelry, which she masterfully refashioned and sold at local synagogues and schools, advertising that the proceeds would be donated to the Solar Cooker Project. The response was overwhelming. Local school parents and community members donated old jewelry and bought the redesigned jewelry. Shelby raised over forty thousand dollars for the Solar Cooker project. Darfuri women are now making 86 percent fewer trips out of refugee camps to collect wood than they were three years ago, with Shelby's help selling her jewelry to the local community.

How did Shelby choose her social action project?

_____

What did she do to include others?

_____

HEBREW HELPER

מַלְבִּישׁ עֲרֻמִּים *(Malbish Arumim)* Clothing the Naked

When Adam and Eve ate from the Tree of Knowledge, they realized they were naked and covered themselves with fig leaves (Genesis 3:7). When Adam and Eve left the Garden of Eden, they needed clothing to wear. According to the Torah, God sewed garments of animal skins for them before they were sent out into the world (Genesis 3:21). In our day, there are many people who cannot afford proper shoes, coats, or eyeglasses. By collecting, distributing, or mending clothing and personal effects, we, too, can perform valuable social actions.

Reflections

In this workshop you learned how to set a timetable, recruit volunteers, and create publicity. Your work plan is in place and you are on your way to beginning your project or initiative.

In anticipation of action, reflect on the following questions.

What aspect of your project is most exciting?

_____

_____

How can you share that excitement with others?

_____

_____

What aspects of your project are you most nervous about?

_____

_____

What can you do to overcome this nervousness?

_____

_____

How will you know you have succeeded in your project?

_____

_____

Doing and Assessing Your Project

Objectives

By the end of this workshop you will be able to:

- Complete your social action project.
- Articulate the importance of evaluation.
- Evaluate your project based on focused questions.
- Describe ways to publicize your accomplishments.

Lesson Launch: ACT! How Are You Doing?

There are three parts to the Social Action Cycle: PLAN, ACT, and EVALUATE. The first three workshops in this manual discussed how to plan your social action project or initiative. Workshop 4 covered the final stages of planning and launched you into action. Now, you should be on your way with your project.

IT'S HAPPENING!

All of the hard work you put into planning your project is about to pay off. To help you share the excitement describe three aspects of your project that are going really well:

1. _____

2. _____

3. _____

As you proceed, remember these aspects, and how much you've accomplished.

EXPECT THE UNEXPECTED

In every project there are bound to be unexpected situations that could impede your progress, such as a delayed meeting or a volunteer who doesn't arrive.

Have you experienced any obstacles? If so, what were they?

_____

_____

DEALING WITH DISAPPOINTMENT

Even if you are feeling frustrated, try to remain flexible. If you have fewer volunteers than you expected, think of creative ways to adjust the work to fit the people who are there. Here are a few tips for dealing with some of these issues:

- *Not enough volunteers?* Scale down the project.

- *Too many volunteers?* Form teams to collaborate on single aspects of the project.

- *Volunteers seem disengaged or detached?* Create excitement by making up songs about the experience, or designate "cheer leaders" to build up morale and encourage everyone to keep working.

- *Experiencing a delay?* Host a discussion about the importance of the work or what Judaism says about it. Bring in this manual and teach a piece of sacred text.

What are other creative solutions to your challenges? Write them here:

_____

_____

In this workshop you will learn how to evaluate your project or initiative, thank your partners and volunteers properly, and tell others what you accomplished.

Focus on Text

וַיַּרְא אֱלֹהִים כִּי־טוֹב . . . וַיַּרְא אֱלֹהִים אֶת־כָּל־אֲשֶׁר עָשָׂה . . .
וְהִנֵּה־טוֹב מְאֹד.

...And God saw that it was good... And God saw all that God created and behold it was very good.

—*Genesis 1:10, 1:31*

In the Torah's account of the Creation of the world, God paused at the conclusion of each day, looked upon what God created, and called the creation "good." We might see God as the original evaluator. The Holy One took into account all that was created, weighed its merits and demerits, and concluded that it was good.

When God created humanity on the sixth day of creation, God said, "This is very good." Why does God's evaluation improve after the creation of human beings? One answer is that God did not create the world perfectly. God needs partnership in perfecting the world. God did not say, "This is perfect." God only said of Creation, "good," and of human beings, "very good."

By doing social action, we partner with God in perfecting the world. Describe a time that you felt like God's partner.

_____

_____

In the same way that God paused after each step of Creation to evaluate it and say, "This is good," we should also pause and assess our social action projects or initiatives. By doing this we make sure that we did our best, even if it is not perfect.

EVALUATE!

During the PLAN and ACT phases of the cycle there were small breaks for assessment. The evaluation in this phase assesses how successful you were at achieving your goals and measures the impact of your project.

KEEP IT TIMELY

Do the evaluation within a few days of the project or initiative. This keeps the experience fresh in your mind and in the minds of others, and maintains a good level of energy and momentum. Schedule about an hour for the evaluation. This keeps the conversation lively and respects the time of your volunteers.

TEAMWORK

In order to include multiple viewpoints, it is best to complete an evaluation with a partner or small group. If you're doing your evaluation with a small group, assign roles to people before you start. You can assign the roles yourself or allow people to volunteer for a position. Either strategy is fine, but be sure to take other people's feelings into account if you are assigning the roles yourself. The roles are:

- **Facilitator:** This person leads the evaluation, keeps the conversation moving along, and is responsible for keeping each person on task.
- **Recorder:** He or she takes notes of the evaluation.
- **Time Keeper:** He or she keeps the evaluation on schedule by tracking time.

THREE BIG QUESTIONS

There are three big questions to answer when evaluating:

1. Did you do what you said you would do?
2. In what ways did your project or initiative have impact?
3. In what ways did the outcome exceed or fail to meet your expectations?

If you can answer all three of these questions, then you will have a complete picture of your project or initiative. The following exercises will help you to focus on each of these three big questions.

1. Did you do what you said you would do?

Rabbi Zusya of Hanipol said, "When I die and go to the world to come, they will not ask me, Zusya, why were you not Moses? They will ask me: Zusya, why were you not Zusya?" (From *Tales of the Ḥasidim*, Martin Buber)

Rabbi Zusya teaches us that we should not expect ourselves to be on the level of Moses, but that we should each be the best person we can be. Ask yourself whether you generally accomplished what you hoped to achieve. Look back at the previous workshops where you wrote down your goals, along with an account of the action taken during your project or initiative.

The goals were: _____

_____

The plan for achieving the goals was: _____

_____

The actual project was: _____

_____

Did you do what you said you were going to do? Explain. _____

_____

2. In what ways did your project or initiative have impact?

The rabbis teach us that Judaism is not just a religion of beliefs but also of actions. To be a Jew is to imitate the actions of God. Just as God feeds the hungry, so should we; just as God clothes the naked, so should we; and just as God lifts up the downtrodden, so should we (Babylonian Talmud, Sotah 16a).

To answer the question about your impact, retrieve any data that you have from your project that can help measure impact. Here are some guiding questions.

Did you raise money? If so, how much? $_____

How many people did you help? _____

How many people volunteered? _____

How many people know about the issue because of the work you did?

_____

Did you inspire anyone to continue to volunteer? If so, whom?

_____

Taking all of these answers into account, how would you say that your project
or initiative had impact? _____

_____

_____

_____

3. In what ways did the outcome exceed or fail to meet your expectations?

In the Torah, Moses told his father-in-law, Jethro, everything that happened to
the Israelites as they left the land of Egypt (Exodus 18). Moses' detailed account
would have included the plagues, the hardened heart of Pharaoh, the preparation
of the matzah, and the splitting of the sea. Moses was careful to relate every
detail as he evaluated the experience of the Exodus and prepared the Israelites
to receive the Torah at Mount Sinai.

Look at every aspect of your project or initiative and answer the following
questions to give yourself the big picture. To answer these questions correctly, be
sure to recall all aspects of your planning process and the actions you took.

General:
Which aspects of the project or initiative were most effective?

_____

Which aspects were least effective?

_____

Volunteers:
Did the volunteers come on time and stay the whole time?

_____

Did you have too many volunteers, too few, or the right number?

_____

Communication:
Did everyone know what they needed to do?

_____

Were there gaps in communication? If so, where?

_____

Materials:
What materials did you have in place before the project began? Were there any that weren't necessary?

_____

What materials were missing that you could have used?

_____

Thank-You Letters:
In addition to celebrating with your volunteers, write a thank-you letter to everyone who partnered with you, contributed their energy, or otherwise helped you with your project. *Do not use e-mail.* Writing a personal thank-you letter and sending it through the mail adds a personal touch that people appreciate. Use the following worksheet to help you construct meaningful thank-you letters.

(Your Address)
(Date)

Dear _____,

Thank you for all of your hard work on my social action project. Together we were able to....

(Insert some of the outcomes of your project here, especially those parts you want to highlight to the person to whom you are writing.)

_____

_____

We could not have accomplished so much without your help.

(Add a sentence about what *specifically* this person did or provided for your project, and how useful this assistance was.)

_____

_____

I hope to be able to work with you on future projects. Again, thank you for your time.

Sincerely,

(Your Name)

CELEBRATE!

Mazal tov! By completing your social action project or initiative you really accomplished something special. Use this space to write your thoughts about how the project went.

_____

_____

_____

_____

_____

_____

GET THE WORD OUT (AGAIN)

Now that you have finished your evaluation and your thank-you letters, it is important to tell others about your success. That way, you can rally more people to your cause and look for additional opportunities to help the community.

There are a number of strategies that you can use for publicity. Write a short paragraph describing your project or initiative, including information about you, the date of your project, and some of your accomplishments. If you include a story of your or someone else's experience as a volunteer, your audience might be more interested in the project and feel more inclined to listen to your message. Look back at your publicity materials and at your evaluation to gather the stories and data about how many people you helped and then use the following space to write your paragraph:

_____

_____

_____

_____

_____

_____

PUBLICITY CHECKLIST

Below is a list of possibilities for publicizing your project or initiative. Check those that interest you and add your own publicity ideas.

❏ Write an article for your school or synagogue newsletter.

❏ Post your success on a blog related to your issue.

❏ Send photographs of your project in action, as well as detailed descriptions, to a local newspaper.

❏ Update your Facebook or MySpace page to reflect the success of your project or initiative.

❏ Ask to speak at a school assembly.

❏ Ask to speak from the *bimah* during synagogue services.

❏ Ask your friends and volunteers to help with publicity by writing or speaking about your project or initiative.

❏ Other ideas:_____

_____

_____

_____

_____

_____

Matthew Rich, Tree Planter Extraordinaire

When Matthew Rich, sixteen, saw a forest of walnut trees in his neighborhood of Concord, North Carolina, razed to make way for a housing development, he decided he needed to act. With sixty dollars of his own money he established a non-profit organization called the Woodland and Wildlife Restoration Committee (WWRC). The WWRC set a goal of planting one thousand trees in the local community. Matthew began his campaign with a garage sale and raised enough money to plant just eight trees.

Two months later Matthew's organization got the attention of the local newspaper, which featured it in a front-page article. Within days, the WWRC raised two thousand dollars from concerned private donors. Matthew then sought and won several matching grants from nonprofit organizations, as well as county and state agencies, to support the WWRC. The International Paper Company offered to donate one thousand trees to Matthew's cause. After evaluating his progress, Matthew realized that he had the money for the trees, but nowhere to plant them. He solicited the local government to use Frank Liske Park, a park near Concord that 170,000 people visit annually. After listening to his request and learning about his backing by the nonprofit and business sectors, the government agreed to let Matthew use the land to plant his forest.

Over time, Matthew convinced his family, friends from the local Boy Scout chapter, and his high school to help him plant the trees. Through his efforts more than two hundred volunteers participated in the project. Ten months after he began his initiative, Matthew planted his thousandth tree.

What steps did Matthew take to publicize his initiative?

_____

_____

Who helped Matthew?

_____

_____

WORKSHOP 5

HEBREW HELPER

בַּל תַּשְׁחִית *(Bal Tashḥit)* **Protecting the Environment**

Armies usually cause terrible destruction during battles and long sieges, but in Deuteronomy 20:19-20, God commands the Israelites not to destroy *(lo tash ḥit)* their enemies' fruit trees. This principle is called *bal tashḥit*. The twelfth-century Jewish thinker Maimonides used *bal tashḥit* to forbid useless destruction in any situation (Mishnah Torah, Melachim 6:8,10). Since then, the rabbis have expanded the commandment to include all environmental considerations. In modern times, *bal tashḥit* has become an important commandment for all Jews who care about the environment. It has become the Hebrew phrase that Jews use to mean, "reduce, reuse, recycle."

Reflections

In this workshop you learned how to evaluate your project and explored strategies for telling others about it. Reflect on your experience by answering the following questions:

In planning and executing your social action project what new information did you learn about your social issue?

_____

_____

Did you learn anything about your own perceptions or opinions by doing a social action project? If so, what? (For example, did you identify stereotypes that influence the way you interact with others, or did you feel less or more excited about working on this social issue than you thought you would?)

_____

_____

What was most challenging about being the leader on this initiative? What was the most rewarding? How do these match your responses in "Who Am I?" on page 15?

_____

_____

Living a Life of Social Action

Objectives

By the end of this workshop you will be able to:

■ Sustain your group of volunteers.

■ Identify chances for social action every day.

■ Commit to a life of social action.

Lesson Launch: A Full Jewish Life

Rank the following Jewish activities in order from most important to you to least important.

Jewish Activities	My order of importance
a) Going to services	1.
b) Celebrating Ḥanukkah	2.
c) Attending a Passover seder	3.
d) Performing social action	4.
e) Celebrating Shabbat	5.
f) Taking a trip to Israel	6.
g) Studying Torah or other Jewish subjects	7.
h) Watching Jewish movies	8.
i) Speaking Hebrew	9.
j) Going to a Jewish summer camp	10.
k) Building a sukkah	11.

What is the most important activity on your list? Why?

_____

Where does social action appear on your list? Think about your reasons for ranking it that way.

There are many components to a full Jewish life, including social action. In this workshop you will learn how to incorporate social action into your daily life. You will also learn some tips on how to translate the energy and experience from your social action project or initiative into a sustainable campaign.

Focus on Text

שִׁמְעוֹן הַצַּדִּיק הָיָה . . . אוֹמֵר עַל שְׁלֹשָׁה דְבָרִים הָעוֹלָם עוֹמֵד: עַל
הַתּוֹרָה וְעַל הָעֲבוֹדָה וְעַל גְּמִילוּת חֲסָדִים.

*Shimon the Righteous…said the world is built on three things: Torah, worship,
and acts of loving-kindness.*

. . .שִׁמְעוֹן בֶּן גַּמְלִיאֵל אוֹמֵר עַל שְׁלֹשָׁה דְבָרִים הָעוֹלָם קַיָּם: עַל הַדִּין
וְעַל הָאֱמֶת וְעַל הַשָּׁלוֹם.

*…Shimon ben Gamliel says the world is built on three things: justice, truth,
and peace.*

—*Pirkei Avot 1:2,18*

What is the difference between these two versions of the "pillars" that support
the world? Why do you think they are different?

_____

How are the two versions similar?

_____

How are they different?

_____

Write your own text based on your Jewish values. On what three things do you
think the world should be built?

(Your name) _____ says, "the world is built on three things:

1)_____

2)_____

3)_____

LIVING AS A YOUNG JEWISH ADULT

Now that you have completed a social action project or initiative, imagine what your Jewish life will look like as you get older. Perhaps it will include joining a youth group, teaching as a *madrich* in a Hebrew school classroom, or participating in your college's Hillel. Living a Jewish life also includes living a life that reflects the Jewish value of *ḥesed*—"loving-kindness."

Read the following scenarios and decide how you might respond using some of the skills you have learned in the previous workshops.

Your local college campus does not use biodegradable paper cups or paper plates in the cafeteria.

_____

_____

On your way to school, you notice a man who appears to be homeless asking for money to buy food.

_____

_____

In your current affairs class, you learn that orphans in Ethiopia typically live in substandard conditions and without proper education.

_____

_____

After speaking with friends, you realize that newer immigrants to your community are having a hard time with classes and making friends in school because they do not know English.

_____

_____

SOCIAL ACTION ANYTIME

Social action can be done in almost any place at any time. The following are some helpful tips for doing social action in as little as a minute or as long as a year. Circle the ideas that interest you and add your own.

Social Action in....

1 Minute

- Wear a t-shirt or button that makes a statement.
- Sign a petition.
- Recycle your soda can.
- Your idea:_____

5 Minutes

- Raise awareness of an issue on campus through publicity.
- Register to vote; help others register to vote.
- Join a social action listserv.
- Send an e-mail to members of your city council or members of Congress about an issue that concerns you.
- Your idea:_____

15 Minutes

- Post informational flyers.
- Post on a listserv or blog about an issue.
- Collect change from friends at the lunch table to donate to charitable organizations.
- Use the internet to calculate your carbon footprint.
- Your idea:_____

30 Minutes

- Present an issue to a school club or synagogue group (sisterhood, social action committee, or executive board).
- Write a letter to the editor of your campus newspaper.
- Plant a tree in an urban community.
- Meet with a campus administrator, school board member, or local community organization to advocate for your issue.
- Tutor someone who cannot read.
- Your idea:_____

1 Hour

- Participate in a rally.
- Take a walking tour of your neighborhood with a community activist.

- Volunteer at a food pantry, soup kitchen, hospital, or women's shelter.

- Write and mail a letter to your representatives or senators.

- Host a discussion group about your issue.

- Your idea:_____

1 Day

- Check the environmental soundness of your home.

- Host an "adopt a pet" day at your school or synagogue.

- Join a local team of volunteers to build houses for the poor.

- Clean a local beach, river bed, or park.

- Dedicate a Shabbat to educating your classmates or congregation about an issue.

- Your idea:_____

1 Week

- Participate in a week of activities to raise awareness about a particular issue.

- Volunteer for a spring/winter/summer break volunteer program.

- Perform an energy audit for your school or synagogue.

- Dedicate a week to raising money for a social issue like domestic violence or child poverty.

- Your idea:_____

1 Month

- Organize your own social action initiative in your school or synagogue. Include service projects, rallies, and fundraising.

- Spend part of a summer volunteering with a community organization.

- Organize a speaker series or film festival about a social issue.

- Build a community garden.

- Your idea:_____

1 Year

- Organize local communities to fight against injustice.

- Create a learning theme for your school or synagogue that reflects a particular social issue such as, "Judaism and Caring for the Elderly."

- Reduce the carbon footprint of your home/school/synagogue through multiple projects and educational programs.

- Create your own nonprofit organization dedicated to a particular issue, like helping to plant trees in your city or improving literacy rates.

- Your idea:_____

TOWARD SUSTAINABILITY

Think of all the work you did to create your social action project or initiative. You created a program, gathered volunteers, and did publicity. By understanding social action as a cycle, you can take the time and energy you put into your project or initiative and direct it toward another project. When you can use your experience as a social action leader to sustain a group of volunteers and promote larger and further-reaching projects or initiatives, then your actions are considered *sustainable*. Here are a few questions and answers that can help you move toward sustainability.

Membership:

Q: How will you increase the number of participants and volunteers for your project? How will you keep your volunteers interested?

A: Make volunteers feel encouraged and needed. Tell them how they can continue to help. People will lose interest if they are not given opportunities to act.

Leadership:

Q: Who will be the new leader or leaders when you or other leaders move on?

A: Look for others who are as passionate about the social issue as you are. Start giving them responsibilities in areas of the project or initiative that foster their own creativity and passions.

HELPFUL TIPS

- *Go monthly:* Change your one-time project into a monthly program by using your new relationships with others in your community.

- *Expand your horizons:* Set a higher fundraising goal or increase the number of people you hope to serve, then work to achieve that goal.

- *Share the wealth:* Change your volunteers into leaders by working together to choose another issue that they can work to address with their own social action initiative.

- Always remember the Social Action Cycle: PLAN, ACT, and EVALUATE.

Social Action Notebook: Building for the Future

Use the following worksheet to help you think about your future doing social action.

Do you think you can commit to doing social action in the future? If so, how can you take your project or initiative to the next level?

_____

_____

How can you continue to increase participation in your project or initiative?

_____

_____

What can you do to create new leadership so that the project or initiative grows?

_____

_____

HEBREW HELPER

צַעַר בַּעֲלֵי חַיִּים *(Tza'ar Ba'alei Ḥayim)* Compassion to Living Animals

In the Torah, if your enemy's donkey becomes overburdened by its load, you are to help lift the load off the animal (Exodus 23:5). The rabbis explain that by doing this you are not acting to benefit your enemy, but rather to help relieve the pain of the donkey itself. As Jews, we should always consider how our actions affect other living creatures and strive not to cause them pain. *Tza'ar ba'alei ḥayim* is still important in our day because it reminds us of how to treat pets, raise farm animals, and live in harmony with the natural habitats of the world.

Alyssa, the Animal Protector

When Alyssa Kane turned thirteen, she jumped at the chance to start volunteering at the Animal Rescue League of Boston (ARL). Alyssa had loved animals ever since she was a child but had to wait until her thirteenth birthday to meet the minimum age requirement to volunteer. Alyssa began volunteering a few hours a week helping to clean cages and groom animals. She also convinced her parents to become a foster family for rescued cats. She began by taking one or two kittens home at a time and assisting in their adoption by a new family.

Over time Alyssa was able to give more hours to the ARL and became a leader in the teen education program. Alyssa took animals, including dogs, cats, and horses, to summer camps to educate teenagers about proper animal care and socialization. In 2008 the Humane Society of the United States awarded Alyssa the "Humane Teen of the Year" award for her hours of dedicated volunteerism and advocacy.

Now seventeen, Alyssa is preparing for college and wants to continue her commitment to helping animals. She hopes to use her experience to join an animal response team and eventually help train animals for law enforcement.

How did Alyssa's volunteerism grow over time?

_____

_____

What skills can Alyssa bring from her teen years into her college and work experience?

_____

_____

Reflections

In this workshop you have learned that you can do social action in as little as a minute a day or regularly throughout your life. You also learned how to sustain a group of volunteers beyond a single project or initiative. Now spend a few minutes reflecting on what doing social action has meant to you. What new ideas have you learned through doing social action? What does your project or initiative mean to your community? What parts of the process did you find meaningful? How have you grown by doing social action? Write your thoughts in the space below.

_____

_____

_____

_____

_____

_____

_____

Conclusion

Mazal tov on completing the *Social Action Manual*!

With this handbook you have taken steps to becoming a partner with God in repairing the world.

You have explored Jewish texts, read success stories of teenagers just like you, and learned the skills necessary to successfully plan a social action project or initiative. In the process you have learned something about yourself and what you care about.

You have also learned that teens can be powerful by leading through example. By being a caring, compassionate leader you can motivate others to engage in the process of social action. As you go forward, you can use the lessons you learned in this handbook to further develop your skills as a young leader of the Jewish community.

Please let us know about *your* social action experiences by writing to socialaction@behrmanhouse.com.